MW01122025

A l   H u n

The
Recklessness
of Love

Bawajiganan gaye
Ni-maanedam

Kegedonce Press
2008

Editor: Kateri Akiwenzie-Damm
Publishing Manager: Renee Abram
Managing Editor: Kateri Akiwenzie-Damm
Cover Design: Poirier Communications
Front Cover Image: Nadya Kwandibens
Back Cover Image: Fred Cattroll
Author Portrait: Stephan Hoglund

Published by Kegedonce Press
Cape Croker Reserve
R.R. 5 Wiarton, Ontario
NoH 2To

www.kegedonce.com

Library and Archives Canada Cataloguing in Publication

Hunter Al, 1958-
The recklessness of love – Bawajiganan gaye ni-maanedam / Al Hunter.

Poems.
Title in English and Ojibway; text in English.
ISBN 978-0-9784998-1-5

I. Title. II. Title: Bawajiganan gaye ni-maanedam.
PS8565.U5767R43 2008   C811'.6   C2008-904645-5

Kegedonce Press gratefully acknowledges the support of:

ONTARIO ARTS COUNCIL
CONSEIL DES ARTS DE L'ONTARIO

Canada Council
for the Arts

Conseil des Arts
du Canada

Distributed by Lit-Distco
100 Armstrong Avenue
Georgetown, Ontario Canada L7G 5S4
Tel: 1 800 591 6250
Fax: 1 800 591 6251

In memory of Sam Visser
a Dylan fan, a poet's friend

May you stay forever young

The *Recklessness* of *Love*

Contents

A Faraway Star

Gazing
At the center
Of a blue violet
In the window box
In the rain
Until it becomes a faraway star

A faraway star
A rainy April night

Without you.

Misfit

A misfit's love for an unattainable lover:
The shoe on the wrong foot.

A river flowing this way

a river flowing this way
here and there and back again
songs and memories
beneath the rise and fall of waves
songs and memories
shelter them and shelter them and shelter them
in your water-laden arms,
in your birth water
shelter them and shelter them and shelter them
upon your shores.

A Flower

A flower at your nipple
My tongue, a wet petal

A Secret of Birds

I wanted to kiss you

To reach out and gently cup your face
And will you

Past our unspoken pause of years
Our widening desire
As the years encircle us

For years, like birds, we rode imperceptible kettles of wind
Aloft and soaring
Sometimes pulled nearer
On subtle swoops and fly-bys
A sky dance of wind and wings
Sometimes pulled afar
In migrations that followed separate stars and constellations
Only to migrate here again
Softly singing memory songs of return and longing

Finally, free of our unspoken pause of years
Finally, reaching across feather-light and closing the distance
Your face gently cupped in wings
Desire fluttered and hovered - hesitation
We alight softly together, we . . .
Finally, ah . . . your mouth, your mouth, your lips, ever so slightly parted
Finally, yes . . . my mouth, on your mouth, our lips softly parting
Again, yes, yes, again . . . please . . . again
Slowly, tenderly we press our mouths together
Yes, tenderly, like hungry birds
Wanting to linger, lest it be our one and only, our last
And then, then,
To take wing, to take wing,
And soar . . .

Silent Mantra

Returning home means
Passing bridges, rivers and old pines
Memories of your smile,
A lock of your hair.

Each time, a silent mantra:
Forgive me, forgive me
After all these years.

Another Fucked-Up Lonely Poem

Right now, right here,
I'm so fucking lonely,
It's fucking me up,
But good.
"No matter," I'm told, "the important thing is
You are not alone."
Lonely but not alone –
How fucked up is that?

Another One Of Those Skeletons In The Closet

Reaching out with hands of bone,
bleached bare and barren of skin,
reaching out, only scratching the surface,
pointing bony fingers to an empty chest,
motioning thirstily to parched, exposed remains,
for a thirst that can never be quenched,
for an empty cage,
which no escape could ever sate,
which no escape could ever sate,
which no escape could ever sate.

Another One Of Those Near-Death Experiences

I'm having another one of those near-death experiences

The kind where snow snakes freeze inside my veins

The kind where ice forms on my eyelids and freezes my eyeballs

The kind where frostbite blackens my heart

The kind where snow drifts against my barren soul

The kind where wind howls inside my hollow ears

The kind where silence is my voice

The kind where there is no tunnel of light

The kind where darkness prevails,

where numbness is my sensation of choice,

where disassociation lifts me above and beyond into the cold, cold comfort of flight.

Cool and Sunny

cool and sunny
a disposition
perhaps a comment
on the weather
maybe just small talk

cool and sunny
a thin sheen of November ice
gathers at the edge of the river
creates fractured light
as clouds pass between the sun and earth.

Dancing Flowers

two blue ones

dance

sway

swoon

sometimes touch

Dream Hotel

I want to do everything with you

You said to me in a dream
As you searched for my mouth
Before taking me onto the bed
Climbing on top of me
Our clothes still on
Our bodies making contact especially through our jeans
When you straddled me
The gathering heat between your legs
Nestled on my balls and on my cock
As our tongues darted and swirled
Inside one another's mouths
Wrapping my face in your trembling hands
You kissed me full and deep
I ran my hands down your ribcage
Over, across and down your back
Putting my hands beneath your blouse
To feel your skin
To run my hands down to your hips
Managing to slip my hands into your jeans
To feel your ass, to squeeze and pull you ever so slightly onto my stiffened cock
To feel you increase the pressure and the tempo of your moistened cunt
Our laboured, excited breathing giving way
Mewling and moans escaping softly
Squeezing and teasing you
Licking, probing and sucking you, soaking your blouse with the wetness
of my mouth
Pulling your blouse open until your buttons pop

The cups of your bra down and over
I draw your swelling nipples in and suck
I pinch and pull, pinch and pull, lick and probe, and suck you
I quicken my tongue and flutter
I grab your ass and pull you
You suck my tongue into your mouth
I suck your tongue into mine
We cannot stifle the moment; we cannot stop the waves from crashing the walls
Our temporal barriers no match against the coming waves that swell and overwhelm
Leaving us awash and panting, until the wetness seeps our jeans

I want to do everything with you
You said to me in a dream

I want to do everything with you
I said to you in a dream

A dream where we could . . .

The way dreams are -
At the dream hotel.

Dream Hotel II

I want to taste you

Your answer is to cup my face in your hands
To wrap your fingers in my hair and pull my mouth to yours

Let me taste you

My answer is to run my tongue sideways until
Your mouth opens
To suck your bottom lip and then your top
To lick your chin
To trace a line of wetness along your jaw line and down
To breathe hot, to lick, flicker, and trace my tongue
To your neck, your throat
Yes, arch slightly, let me lick your neck, let me gently bite, let me gently suck
Yes, let me . . .
You arch, and urge me, your fingers in my hair
To that ridge inside your clavicle
To lick that tiny moist cup between your neck and shoulder
To lick along the collar of your blouse and skin
To follow that tiny, salty trickle between your breasts
And back around and over to the caps of your nipples
Hardening, shining, beneath the slickness of my tongue
Tracing a flat, wet trail around your darkening areolas
Made darker by my exploring, wet mouth
Back and around, and circling, and circling, the swelling wetness that becomes
my well,I drink at the trickle that gathers at your breastbone

I must taste you

Our answer is to breathe deep when my tongue reaches your belly
Heaving slightly, our fingers coiled in sheets, our breath caught in the heat of
moments Moments delve into minutes, that delve into my mouth that delve
onto my tongue
that delve into the first inviting wisps of you . . .

Yes, taste me . . .

Dream Hotel IV
learning by heart

Before the fingers of first light parts curtains
I wake beside you
I gaze upon you
Your back faces me
Your hip rests on sheets of violet
Your legs entwined ever so slightly

Closing my eyes
I will my hands to learn by heart, your map of contours
Your geography
I trace an invisible trail from your feet
To your ankles, to your calves, pausing to trace small circles,
Markers to find my way back
Your terrain begins a gentle slope at your thighs
After the forget-me-not cusp behind your knees

Pausing again to imagine the gentle slopes of your thighs
The elevation that softly rises at your hips beckons my hands
To keep climbing, then to rappel downward slowly
Along the perfect symmetry of your ass
Down, down and under slightly, then, up
To your lower spine
I am a blind man seeing with my trembling fingertips
Descending the slope of your hip
Finding your ribcage, rappelling again slowly down the soft heat of your back
An ascending climber to the undulating ridge of your arm
Down and up again
To the sheer drop of your shoulder
Resisting the urge to plummet, to surrender to the softness of your neck
Descending slowly, then, up
To run my fingers through your hair, and, over
Tracing to your chin, your mouth, your cheek, and down again

You stir, whispering

Oh . . .

Shhhhhhh, let me, love, let me . . .

Turning onto your back, you whisper and murmur

Yes, love me . . .

First light whispers back onto the undulations and curves of your body
To elucidate the coming journey
That I first traced with fingertips, feather-light

To trace again with my mouth and light kisses
To retrace yet again with my tongue
To drink of rivulets and streams, dew and surge

At every nook and cranny
Lush valley, crevice, and meadow

Willingly, I begin at your feet again
Unhesitant I journey
My recompense to you

I learn by heart.

I am your wayward fool.

Feathers

on the winds
in the willows
on the waters
in the skies
finding their way to here
to there
to you
to me.

Ghosts at Big Sur

I went to Big Sur to look up Brautigan, only to have someone tell me he was dead. "Yea, Brautigan is dead, man. Shot himself in '84." Well, disappointed, shocked and feeling more than a little silly for not knowing Richard was dead, for not knowing what I should have known, I decided to go to Big Sur anyway. I was going to reconnoiter with his ghost. Yea, I heard tell of a cave along the California coast that local legend said bore the bloodied shaky handprints of Richard Brautigan himself, blown onto the cave wall from the last thunderous shot that left a bloody poetic hole in the world.

Along the way, I met Dylan. Bob, that is, carrying on at the side of the road, strumming a guitar, singing one of his signature tunes, near Fresno, that shriveling heart of the desert. I said, "Bob, you might be interested to know that I'm going up to the Big Sur coast in search of Richard Brautigan's ghost. Wanna come along?" Damned, if Bob said, "Yea," He says," He always was one for words." "Did you know he shot himself years ago," I ask Bob. "Yea," says Bob, "there was blood in the sky when Brautigan died." "I guess it was overcast where I happened to be that day." I muttered. I could only feign silence. My breath gave me away. "I didn't know." I thought to myself.

Bob and me talked about the growing disconnection between the poetics of the soul and of the mind. We talked about how music and the soul, poetry and suffering, music and redemption, storytelling and healing, were necessarily tethered to the same cosmic bird of the universe, man. We talked about the messages and messengers of music and poetry and how, why, did it always have to end up feeling so forlorn and lonely all the time?

I said, "I don't know, Bob. That's one for heaven's door." Bob didn't say anything. I thought he might think that was clever of me to draw a reference to one of his own works. If he did, he wasn't going to say. Maybe because it may have sounded like I was just making fun, which I wasn't.

We traveled along in silence for a while above and through the foothills, through the gusty valleys, and through warm kettles of wind, red-tailed hawks and kites, catching glimpses of the sparkling and pulsing sea.

"We're almost there." I say to Bob. "Yea, it's alright, man. That's what we're lookin' for, babe" "Curious." I think to myself, "Was that a return verbal play on words from Bob because of my earlier wise-ass remark about heaven's door." I decide that it isn't worth pursuing any further. Bob and I had better things to do.

The coast was a rugged, twisting, turning, magnificent, frightening, display of precipice and light, swelling, heaving waves, and frothing, exploding surf. The sea itself was relatively calm. Still, for one more used to swaying pines and shaking poplars, the sea was not to be taken lightly. We had arrived at Big Sur.

Now, I figured that reconnoitering with the ghost of Richard Brautigan was going to require more than a séance of poetry and luck. We needed some wine, some whiskey, maybe some rum, some smokes, and maybe, some weed. Having been a teetotaler for more than half my life at this point, I decide not to let this get in the way of making this journey a waste of time. "Bob, do you think that we could stop at that general store along the way to pick up some wine, whiskey, rum, and, maybe, some smokes?" "Yea," answers Bob, "whatever it takes to get us through the night." "There he goes again," I think silently. Bob has his famous black hat pulled down over his eyes. I can't read anything about that remark right now. "Forget it," I think, and decide to let it go.

"How about some weed?" I ask. Bob doesn't stir beneath his black hat. His thin demeanor would yield no clues one way or the other. I take it as a yes. Dressed in black from head to toe, Dylan is all cool. He is wearing a mid-length black jacket with silver buttons that he has buttoned all the way up and down; two silver buttons punctuate the back where his waist would be. Silver buttons punctuate his black jeans from the sides of his knees to the bottom of his hems. Even his black boots are cool. "I'd love to smoke some weed with you and Brautigan and say I did, Bob," I say to myself. "I'd love to share some wine, a whiskey, straight-up or a shot of rum as a night-cap in a cave lit up with a small fire somewhere with Brautigan and me and you. What a night!" I think silently. Bob still doesn't stir.

Bob intimidates me; his cool intimidates me.

Finally, we continue in our earnest search for Brautigan's ghost, his cave, his company. Let me tell you why I want to talk with Brautigan. I'm lost, man. I need some inspiration. I feel like I'm dying inside. I realize that I made need more than inspiration. I need a reason to go on. I'm hoping that talking with Brautigan will renew the flames of poetic fire and life inside me once again. The irony of going to see a guy who killed himself is not lost on me. Besides, I've loved his poetry for years. Three of his thin volumes of poetry have graced my collection and my world for years: "The Springhill Mining Disaster," "Rommel Drives On Deep Into Egypt" and others. Lines of his poetry have left me haunted: "then to lie silently like deer tracks . . ." and more. Brautigan, that suicidal maniac kept me alive, hopeful, even while his poetry despaired and endured. I was a young man kept alive, vicariously, through his words, his genius, and his pain. "Damn you, Brautigan! How could I ever hope to repay you? Yet, knowing that I cannot make you responsible for this debt I feel is mine unpaid."

The sun beats down on me and Bob descending a topsy-turvy, twisting, winding, rising trail beneath cedars and eucalyptus heavy with scent and sap, over a clear, cold, mountain stream spilling down the craggy rocks and into the waiting mouth of the open sea.

Up and over rocks and boulders, we climb. The waves and surf tossing and swelling in the emerald and jade green sea. We search for Brautigan's cave in silent awe, our breath unabated, and our heaving breath giving us away.

This part we cannot traverse without difficulty, without trepidation, without caution. It dawns on me that I've never asked Bob why he chose to come along, why he wanted to see Brautigan. I'll ply him with him with booze and ganja, I decide silently. "You are a coward," I say beneath a heaving breath. "Just ask him." I decide that I will as soon as there is a moment to catch our breath somewhere on the craggy shore at the foot of this enduring precipice.

"Before we call for Brautigan, we need to sit here for a spell just to let him know that we're here and that we came here to see him," I say to Bob. "Yea, alright," says Bob. I continue, "I just hope we're at the right place, Bob. I hear that guy Henry Miller is supposed to be around here somewhere, too." I pause. "Then again, Miller's ghost is probably somewhere in the deep south or somewhere else just as hot and sultry. Somewhere where men and their ghosts have the option of anonymity, somewhere where they can smoke cigars and sip whiskey in relative obscurity and still enjoy the company of a lover or two, the taste of cigars or whiskey on their ghostly breath, whatever the case may be, without all the pretenses of a polite society. They're ghosts now, after all." Dylan's only response was, "Who's Henry Miller, man?"

Ignoring the question, I begin preparing our altar, our séance of poetry, luck, wine, whiskey, rum, smokes, and ganja in our attempt to lure the ghost of Richard Brautigan, to converse, and, otherwise reconnoiter with two travelers looking for a ghost at Big Sur.

I ask Dylan if he's hungry and if he'd like to split one of the organic, all vegetarian, bean and cheese burritos that I picked up at that general store down the road. I tell him that I brought along an extra one for Brautigan just in case he's hungry, too. Bob nods affirmatively, his black hat tipping in my direction as he leans his thin frame against a large boulder; his guitar leaned gently beside him, sheltered from the sun, the spray from the surf wafting over us like tiny, gossamer, misty threads of sea and grace. We are here to see Brautigan.

I prepare our offerings: my collection of three tattered books of poetry by Brautigan, (ones that I've had since my twenties,) 3 glasses of wine, whiskey and rum, a pack of Lucky Strikes (soft pack), a fat joint of sensimilla; and, of course, the organic, all vegetarian, bean and cheese burritos. I, of course, revere the books that contain some of the finest poems of Brautigan, the very same poetry, that in its genius imagery and metaphors, kept a young man alive, albeit hurting and alive. The booze I see as showing Brautigan that if he wants a good, stiff drink before, during or after, that it's all going to be fine by me. The Luckys are there because smoking and drinking go hand in hand. Besides, tobacco is always a good offering for a ghost. The reefer was simply a guess on my part. There was a chance that it wouldn't be appreciated, though deep down, I doubted that. It seemed like a mellow winner, if you asked me. Bob made no outward, discernible objections at the time of its procurement. The wine, whiskey and the rum would taste sweeter because of it, I was sure. The burritos for the meal and the munchies that would surely accompany any sojourn down the road with ganja and drink.

After all of this placed at the feet of this magnificent precipice, at the awesome mouth of the sea, at the gateway to Brautigan's cave, I ask Dylan if he'd do the honor of playing a song while I attempt to conjure the ghost of Richard Brautigan. He tips his black hat again, places his guitar across his thighs, legs outstretched and crossed, Bob Dylan begins to play, "Knockin' at Heaven's Door." I am awestruck, stunned silent. The notes and the melody wafting over as I utter softly, homages to Brautigan.

The sea kelp bobbed and poked its heads above the waves like peeping sea lions, like emerging spirits from the sea. The wind drew closer in sweeps and arcs, the mist from the surf wafted over, me, and there I was, half expecting Brautigan to appear mist-like, apparition-like from the crashing waves demanding, "Show me the money!" or some such thing. Well, it didn't happen like that.

Instead, just as Bob and I crooned the chorus of his song, my collection of Brautigan's poetry got swept up in a gust of wind and blew into the sea. I said to Bob, "Keep playing!" Next the glasses of wine, whiskey and rum spilled their spirits onto the rocks, until all that was left were the Lucky Strikes, the swollen joint, and the organic, all vegetarian, bean and cheese burritos. "He's here," I say to Bob. He nods his head again and keeps playing.

Dylan and I are silent on our drive south, down the coastal highway. Brautigan never did show up. We waited there on the craggy shore. Bob played his guitar, sang some songs, we ate the burritos, smoked some cigarettes, drank, got high, then munched on Brautigan's share, too. Bob reminded me that sometimes as humans, we make our search for answers longer than it need be, though the distance be short, sometimes right in front of our noses. Brautigan's dead. His poetry lives. You live. Simple.

As I came to a fork in the road, the highway continuing south and also turning east, I slowed the car and came to a stop. I turned to Bob and said, "I'm going head east from here, Bob. I'm gonna head back home." "That's fine with me, friend. I'll get along just fine from here. Maybe I'll head on to San Francisco. Remember what I told you, friend."

"I will" I replied.

Bob took his guitar and sauntered coolly south down the coastal highway. I could hear the words of his song. I watched and listened to him until I couldn't see him anymore.

"May God bless and keep you always, May your wishes all come true,
May you stay forever young, forever young, forever young,
May you stay forever young."

Here I Am

here I am
not knowing
if I am
yellow on
gray
or gray on
yellow
in darkness or
in light
tethered or
winged
Here I am
I know
I am
without you.

Rez Dogs

I am just a rez dog now, I am a refugee
There is no sound, no sound, only the empty sea
It cannot be real, because you are not near
It's just the fog, I fear

We're just all rez dogs now, we're just all refugees

Oh, heaven, where are you now?
There is no sound aglow, no ground, below
The earth destroyed, destroyed, you know
Our deafness it grows and grows

I'm just a rez dog now, I am a refugee
There is no sound, no sound, only the empty sea
I t cannot be real, because you are not near
It's just the fog I fear

We're all just all rez dogs now, we're all just refugees

Oh, promised land, where are you now?
There are no oars aboard, no way ashore
The sky destroyed, destroyed, you know
Our blindness it grows and grows

I'm just a rez dog now, I am a refugee
There is no sound, no sound, only the empty sea
I t cannot be real, because you are not near
It's just the fog I fear

We're all just all rez dogs now, we're all just refugees

Oh, freedom, where are you now?
There are no bells to peal, no anchor to weigh
The water destroyed, destroyed, you know
Our thirst it grows and grows

I'm just a rez dog now, I am a refugee
There is no sound, no sound, only the empty sea
I t cannot be real, because you are not near
It's just the fog I fear

We're all just all rez dogs now, we're all just refugees

Oh, love, where are you now?
There are no thorns to feel, no petals to pull
The air destroyed, destroyed, you know
Our muteness, it grows and grows

I'm just a rez dog now, I am a refugee
There is no sound, no sound, only the empty sea
I t cannot be real, because you are not near
It's just the fog I fear

We're all just all rez dogs now, we're all just refugees

Oh, desire, where are you now?
There are no flames to tend, no warmth to send
The light destroyed, destroyed you know
Our silence, it grows and grows

I'm just a rez dog now, I am a refugee
There is no sound, no sound, only the empty sea
I t cannot be real, because you are not near

It's just the fog I fear

We're all just all rez dogs now, we're all just refugees

I have been to war

I honor your gods,
I drink at your well.
I bring an undefended heart to
our meeting place.
I will not negotiate by withholding.
I will not be held captive by
disappointment.

- Ralph Blum

I have been to war
I have touched the faces of death
They have touched me
I have scorched the hands of death
They have scorched me
They have smothered me.

breathe
struggle
gasp
run
escape

I have been
captured
tortured
bound
I have been
I have been
I have been
I have been

"it's ok, it's ok, it's ok."
"the more you struggle . . ."
"the more it will hurt . . ."
"it will hurt . . ."
"no one can hear you."
"no one can hear you."
"no one can hear you."
"stop kicking."
"stop kicking."
"stop kicking."
"no one can hear you."
"no one can hear you."
"no one can hear you."

I know the birds are there,
there, in the trees.
I know the clouds are there,
there, in the sky.
I know the winds are there,
there, in my hair.
I know the earth is there,
there, somewhere.
I know the waters are there,
there, there, there, & there.

My nest, my recovery place,
my hiding place, my resting place,
my nesting place, my crawling space,
my crying place, my wounded place,
my cleansing place, my cleansing place, my cleansing place.

"where are you, birds?"
"where are you, trees?"
"where are you, clouds?"
"where are you sky?'
"where are you, wind?"
"where are you, earth?'
"where are you, you?'
"where are you, waters?'
"where, where, where?"
"where are you?"
"where, where, where?"

"where are you, boy?"

"I'm telling you, that's the way it happened."

I have been to war
I have been the faces of death
I have touched you
I have been the scorched hands of death
I have scorched you
I have smothered you

breathe
struggle
gasp
run
escape

I have
captured
tortured
bound
you

I have
I have
I have
I have

"it's ok, it's ok, it's ok."
"the more you struggle . . ."
"the more it will hurt . . ."
"it will hurt . . ."
"no one can hear you."
"no one can hear you."
"no one can hear you."
"stop kicking."
"stop kicking."
"stop kicking."
"no one can hear you."
"no one can hear you."
"no one can hear you."

"I'm telling you, that's the way it happened."

"where are you, boy?"
"inside the man, where are you?"
"inside the boy, where are you?"
"inside, where are you?"
"where are you?"
"where, are you?"
"where?"
"where?"
"are you?"
"are you?"
"you?"
"you?"
"you?"
"you."

"I'm telling you, that's the way it happened."

I have been to war
I have touched the faces of death
They have touched me
I have scorched the hands of death
They have scorched me
They have smothered me

breathe
struggle
gasp
run
escape

I have been
captured
tortured
bound

I have been
I have been
I have been
I have been

"its ok, it's ok, it's ok."

"the more you tell . . ."

"the less it will hurt . . ."

"it won't hurt . . ."

"I can hear you."

"I can hear you."

"I can hear you."

"I can hear you."

"start kicking . . ."

"start kicking . . ."

"start kicking . . ."

"We can hear you."

"We can hear you."

"We can hear you."

"We can hear you."

"We hear you."

"That's the way it happened."

"where are you, boy?"

I have been to war
and back.
I am dreaming
beyond the nightmares.
I have been to war
and back.
I am healing
beyond the trauma.
I have been to war
and back.
I am listening
beyond those voices.
I have been to war
and back.
I am reaching
beyond the bondage.
I have been to war
and back.
I am singing
beyond the stars.
I have been to war
and back.

I am singing

I am singing
I am singing
I am singing
I am singing
beyond bird's wings
beyond outstretched fingers
beyond swirling clouds
beyond crushing blue skies
beyond whirling winds
beyond confines of earth
beyond bloodied waters
beyond you & you & you & you.

"where are you, boy?"

We have been to war
and back.
We are dreaming
beyond the nightmares.
We have been to war
and back.
We are healing
beyond the trauma.
We have been to war
and back.
We are listening
beyond those voices.
We have been to war
and back.
We are reaching
beyond the bondage.
We have been to war
and back.
We are singing
beyond the stars.
We have been to war
and back.

We are singing

We are singing
We are singing
We are singing
We are singing
beyond birds' wings
beyond outstretched fingers
beyond swirling clouds
beyond crushing blue skies
beyond whirling winds
beyond confines of earth
beyond bloodied waters
beyond & beyond & beyond & beyond.

"I hear you."

I sing your praises.
You sing mine . . . .

"We hear you."

We sing your praises.

You sing ours . . . .

If your love is a 50 calibre machine gun
Fresno, CA, Oct 2004

If your love is a 50 calibre machine gun, baby
Then assassinate me
If your love can pierce armour, baby
Then assassinate me
If your heart is a minefield,
Then, baby, assassinate me
If your heart is a hand grenade,
Baby, then, assassinate me
If your soul can level mountains, baby
Then assassinate me
If your soul can shock and awe
Then, baby, assassinate me
If your body is a sleeper cell
Then, baby, assassinate me
If your body is a bomb
Then, baby, assassinate me
Assassinate me, baby
Assassinate me, baby
Assassinate me, baby
Baby, assassinate me.
If your eyes are skies on fire, baby
Then assassinate me
If your lips are the kiss of death, baby
Then assassinate me
I hear the rat-a-tat-tat
I hear the explosions, baby
I hear the rat-a-tat-tat
I hear the explosions, baby
I feel the earth shakin', baby

I feel the earth shake
I see the flames burnin', baby
I see the flames burn
I taste your loving cyanide, baby
I taste your sweet death.
Assassinate me, baby
Baby, assassinate me
Baby, assassinate me.
If you got me in your sights
Then, pull the trigger, baby
Assassinate me.

My whole life going home

One beautiful evening in June, I met an Aleut woman in the
small dining room of an old elegant hotel. We were two Indians
in Washington, DC, each having dinner alone. We nodded
to one another across the room the way Indians do, a silent
acknowledgement and an invitation. After introductions, we
shared a table. While the waiter brought us water, appetizers
and entrée's all served elegantly, she told me of windswept arctic
islands, the islands she and the Aleut people called home.

"I've spent my whole life going home," she said.

Kindred Spirits
For my Saami brothers & sisters

I

Beneath an autumn moon, a peak rises out of the northern shores
of Lake Superior.
"Who else calls this valley home,
this valley of memories and kindred spirits?

II

In October
at dawn it seemed
cold enough to crack teeth.
Frost covered the meadow below and the hillside above.
We need to be up there before sunrise. I tell my companions.
We are going to greet the sun from that hill.
Making our way through frost and cold in silence,
the peak rose before us in the stillness, in the warming hands
of first light.

At the pinnacle, in a circle of trees,
we prepared to greet the sun.
With the first breath of the pipe,
a circle of birds,
a circle of song.

As the sun rose,
a beam of light danced across the waters,
a voice sounded from the east.

We acknowledged the sun.
We acknowledged the nagamon.

We acknowledged the joik.
We acknowledged the kindred spirits,
singing, coming home. . . .

* *joik prounounced yoik: general translation = song in the Saami language.*
* *nagamon: general translation = song in the Ojibwe language.*

Lacuna

In the hollows between time and forgiveness
In between love and longing.
In the hollows between grace and faith
In between diamonds and the rough.
In the hollows between struggle and freedom
In between flotsam and pearls.
In the hollows between earth and sky
In between anguish and recovery.
In the hollows between darkness and dawn
In between memory and healing.
In the hollows between proof and promises
In the hollows between love and loss
Finding you.

My heart is a wild horse

My heart is a wild horse
Tethered to the clouds.

My heart is a wild horse
Tethered to the clouds.

Tethered nonetheless.

Night Wings

Flying in the light of the moon
Searching for you
Shall we pass one another in the night?

Offering

From her,
I'll take whatever's left over
"Give me the crumbs" I say.

I'll make room.

On the Other Side of the Moon

Medellin, June 2006

Beyond the mountains of Colombia
The moon is hiding
Beyond the Lake of the Sand Hills
My dream lover's eyes.

Out of the Gallows

gossamer threads keep me here
dancing at the edge of grandeur
wobbly faith woven into a precarious grace
gossamer threads keep me here
bound to this earth
this lucid sphere

ragged threads keep me here
dangling at the edge of darkness
between subjugation
and a dark-hooded stranger
ragged threads keep me here
bound to this hell
this tattered diaphone

bound to this earth
this earth
gossamer threads keep me here
keep me
keep me
keep me here
bound to this earth
this earth
this earth
this earth

Portrait of a Pipe Maker
for Bob Morris

He finally saw the sun on the other side
of his long madness
saw his reflection in the eyes
of a black bear
finally shook hands with the man
and accepted his gifts.

This is why
you have held the moon in your hands
wandered the floors of lakes, rivers, streams
speaking with stones
and the dwellers of cliffs and caverns
I am here
I am in this stone
I am alive
I am alive
I am alive
I am the voice of water
A diver of words
lift me to the sky
to the winds
to the earth
to all things living
palm full of tobacco
breath full of prayer
in return I will offer my palm
filled with tobacco
answer your prayer
breathe
breathe
breathe
I will be the eagle praying at dawn . . . .

I saw the sun on the other side
of my long madness
I saw my reflection in the eyes
of a black bear
I finally shook hands with the man
I accepted my gifts . . . .

Scorched Earth Poem

Beyond the scorched earth of my heart
On the other side of gently burning flames
A healing fire
For four days and nights we kept vigil

Over time, over these years, over these winters, over these times
Keeping time with the sun as it rose and set
Keeping time with the moon as it rose and set
Keeping time with this perpetual fire, this one
This one that still burns, this one, this one that still burns
This one that still burns for you.

Our scorched hearts having healed
On the same side as the other of these gently burning flames
Our healing fire
This one that still burns, this one, this one that still burns
This one that still burns for me and for you
This one that still burns for me and for you.

Sugar Bush

My love, I'm going
to the sugar bush today
to turn sap into syrup
– the fire has started –
I will add wood and dip
a balsam
branch into the pot
to take away the steam
to take my time
that's how the sweetest syrup is made
by taking the time
to wait, to stir the sap
to wait and stir, to wait and stir,
to tend the fire,
to dip the balsam,
to take the time,
finally, later
to dip my fingers in and swirl –
to bring it to my mouth, my tongue
and taste . . . ,
so sweet,
so real,
so natural,
so worth the wait. . . .

George's Art of War

Clinging to life,
A fading twilight smears bloodstained fingers
Across the apathetic face of yet another evening sky;

Succumbing to yet another hue of shadows,
Another futile struggle,
Another failed masterpiece.

The Sky

The sky having cleared itself of clutter and cloud,
holds sway over ice clustering in the bay,
above these rapids, on this river flowing west.

As the river opens and swells more and more,
as the crushing, overpowering clatter relents and is quelled
beneath a splendidly blue sky,
beneath a sun that will not shilly-shally,
vigilant and still, two eagles ponder the warming, stilling eddies. . . .

Yes, vigilant and still.

Sequins

A travelling moon
Blue in a nightly traverse
Falling stars slowly surrender
To the winter place
A universe of stars and constellations
Sequined on the snowy belt of earth

The Surgeon of Love

left

a gaping hole
where my heart used to be.

Working Title

warmonger to peacemaker to warmonger
and back again
slave keeper to freedom fighter to slave keeper
and back again
enslavement to liberation to enslavement
and back again
democrat to republican to autocrat to democrat
and back again
sing the song, dance the tune
worship the sun, shoot the moon
drop the ammo, lift the gun
you're not alone, you're not the one

Dreams & Regrets

"It was my destiny I think, to marry who I married. To live the life I'm in. To usher in sadness as if it were my long lost twin. But, I also believe, it is my destiny to know you and I will take that knowledge in whatever form it comes."

- Lisa Zaran

Dear_____:

Last night, on my way back home, I thought about what I wrote to you. I'm sorry.

This isn't easy to say: Most of the time it's about irreconcilable grief and a deep abiding loneliness, the reasons for my meanderings, my wanderings, my propensity for the absurd of amount of solitary time that I need and sometimes loath myself for, in order to feel somewhat sane, sane enough to carry on in this sometimes fucked-up world. Tragic and joyful that it shall never change.

It's easier to think of the possibility that we shall lay next to one another, that we shall hold one another again one day, that we shall again kiss, that we shall shed one another of our clothing in the dark and make mad, raw, tender love for the first, and, perhaps, the last time. It is easier to think of that than it is to think of the probability that it shall never happen like that.

Hence, in a strange way, it's easier to maintain a hidden well of grief and loneliness, than it is to feed the unquenchable thirst of fantasy and dreams and love.

I love you. I know I ask too much of you. There's no reason to consider me. Just, if you can, once in a while, tell me that you still love me, that you miss me, too. That shall be enough water in the well for me to carry on.

Always,

the one who loves you

The Recklessness of Love

I tasted bread and blood.
What more can a poet want?

\- Pablo Neruda

My love, it has been one week since
I've sent you a poem

7 days ago
I swam awkwardly with words
Weighted down with rusting chains and stones

6 days ago
I walked aimlessly with sentences
Past the same trees notched with blood and skin

5 days ago
I ran clumsily in tears
Speaking tongues of rain

4 days ago
I brawled drunkenly with metaphors
Through shards of glass and pain

3 days ago
I dreamed, I dreamed, I dreamed
fire and earth

2 days ago
Words fell like songs in a deep river
like stones

1 day ago
I breathed, I breathed, I breathed
constellations and faith

Here, now, my love, is another dusky star

Reckless love in the language of stone.